THE COLOR BOOK
CREED
VOLUME 2

C. J. HENRY

Published by:

www.owlpublishers.com
360 S Market St, San Jose, CA 95113,
United States.

Printed in the United States of America

DEDICATION

This poetic philosophical masterpiece is dedicated to every version of myself (C.J. Henry). The Good. The Bad. The Ugly. Weaknesses. Strengths. The mysteries and mysteriousness. All the things' women might need to heal, might need for comfort, might need to hear. All of it.

RAW: (Of an emotion or quality) strong and undisguised.
STRONG. INTENSE. PASSIONATE.TRUE TO LIFE...

TABLE OF CONTENTS

PART 1

"The blessing with me is I never have a bad intention. It's always for a reason; like regardless. If the truth is involved, then I'm not even allowed to be worried. It's those that traffic in falsehood. They gotta worry about me."

– Katt Williams

PRECIOUS

Life is precious,
Count your blessings.
In just a blink, don't you think you can't sink.
Hold fast, and keep your head on swivel,
Even if life is on the brink.

Change is our stranger, heartless regardless,
You won't know what to think.

Reach to the heavens and ask GOD to open your mind,
So that you may understand his plan.
Rest assured with him, there's always a safe space to land.

Sojourn in the hour, with the flow is where you're going.
Perceiving the moment while entering the unknown land.
Trust as well as the steps required go hand in hand.
Depths are limitless once you decide that you can.

Life is precious,
Count your blessings.
Karma is but a reflection.

A reflection in a mirror looks back at you.
Mind battles in the shadows, throws attacks at you.
Daggers, trash, and everything but the facts at you.
Pulling down strongholds is your weapon for
everything the devil casts at you.

Believe in yourself!
That's all I ask of you.

Treat it as a task for you.
An everlasting tool,
That separates those who are wise,
And those who are fools.

For every breath you take,
Another life GOD may take.
As the previous day has finished,
Arise into mornings gladly replenished.

Be blessed risen in the morrow, some days may be good
while another's is filled with sorrow.
Humble yourself, don't stumble yourself,

There's no promise for tomorrow,
For nothing is our own.
So, respect the time that is borrowed.
Might I include, appreciate your health and all GOD designed
for our bodies to do, long before doctors had a clue.

A body in good health heals itself from sicknesses,
Be not deceived.
GOD never leaves Himself without witnesses.

During the pandemic, many recovered from the flu,
Though other families grieved, seeing their loved ones being
kept alive by machines and tubes.
It's rude. How crude?
Walking around like
Nightmares aren't just as real as
dreams that come true.

Life is precious.
Count your blessings.

Don't see a lie, but a tie,
This is the nexus.

Lo and behold, my words to you are gold,
Going toe to toe, in the midst,
GOD gets all the glory in my life
As he protects it.

"This is my program. I'm on my time. And I told y'all that last year. And I told y'all that this year. This my shit!"

— Ari Fletcher

DISRESPECTFUL

Disrespect?
That's old news.
Don't you assume, because I appear soft
That this Christian won't come off.

It's like becoming a new creature,
In an instant, you are the same person, just with new
features.
Life is the teacher, Afterall
If you must fall, understand it's all a part of the call.
And with every spring, there is fall.
Where there is disrespect, there is withdrawal.
But, oh no, that's not all.

Did you expect not to be checked?
For a second, it seemed as if you thought you had
forever to not be put with the rest.

My time with you! HA!
Consider the pilgrim passing through.
Oh, how through I am with you.
There isn't any room for you to assume
It's my desire to relive such a test.
So let me say it with my chest.
That's the best!
DISRESPECT?
I HAVE NO PATIENCE LEFT.
Always at peace, doing what's best.
I'm not Lot's wife,
Never look back.
Not once. Not twice.

Looking back will have you stuck like ice.
Looking back, I despise; only the future glistens in my eyes,
Living life with no regrets.

Reject negativity equivocally and initially.
It's all about respect. Honesty. Loyalty.
I can tell by your anger that you can't accept that I'm
royalty.
So rebellious you are. Defiant.
Your vivid attempts to cut me down are how I know
that I'm a giant.
I am where you never go.
My anointing scares you.
You don't think I know.

I abhor hatred; I'll dismiss it from afar.
How could you be so lost in darkness that you reject the light
in this star?
Some people's hearts become hard.
I mean, they could be losing yet allow jealousy to persuade
them to shun my winning cards.
My pride is on the side,
I reach out to help, but here they are attempting to hurt me.
Lord, Have Mercy!
I've picked up my cross to carry you, and you're not even
worthy.
Don't disturb me!

Disrespect?
You see, that could be your greatest disappointment yet.

Though forgiveness is a virtue.
My salvation isn't worth you.
So goodbye!
Don't bat your eyes.
I'm tempted to wish you well.
But all you leave me with is a disappointing sigh!

"She's a phenomenal person. She's a phenomenal talent."

— Keven Sr.

ROME

Like roaming around in space,
Pieces of me fell,
Only to land me in place.

Time presents itself as an understanding to all who choose.
to see, within periods of time,
It inevitably reveals what's underneath.

I'd be bold to say, "truth be told", by the time I'm old or
some humble abode, some fantasy of perfection,
Though my destiny is the best of me, bigger, better,
A light to whoever,
Standing on two,
An overcomer in all I went through.
Open your eyes.

Even when you cry.
Find strength in believing,
Even if your hands are tied.

Loving family and friends are normal deeds,
But those same people may disappoint you,
Others might not be good for you,
and you'll have to tell them goodbye,
not literally, though I'm not speaking soft,
I mean, when someone's bad for you,
You must cut them off. Cut them loose.

Off the grid is isolation.
Slothfulness is hesitation.
Self-care is meditation.

Life is too short
not to put GOD first,
His breath is what gives us life at birth.
His water is living forever, quenching our thirst.
Put yourself first in any situation.

You are like Rome.
Spaces are big and open; ancient,
Both soft and slow, but it's history, irrevocable,
Like our minds at times.
Why not roam?
Why not open our minds?
Why not open our hearts?
Manifesting peace.

Off the grid in Rome, sometimes
Feels like your real home.
Meditation is hibernation,
And high vibrations.
Facts.

In those high vibrations,
You won't chase but attract.
Rome.

What a safe space to be.
The love and peace for or within yourself,
Will be so powerful, you won't want to leave.

"Any friend who turns into an enemy has been hating since day one."

— Tupac Shakur

WHAT YOU CAN SEE

To what measure is hate?
To what are you owed this pleasure?
With a spirit as rich as Lannister wealth.
Like Tyrion, it's clever!
You can tell by the hate when something and someone are
great.
When it's in you, there's no escape.
It doesn't hide or wear a disguise.
That envy. That jealousy. Is always awake!
It's an aura so fierce; it won't have to walk by.
I spy with my little eye, envious souls cursing at the sky.
One glance at your blessings has them wishing they'd go
blind.
I mean, they'll be so casually unkind.

Hate me?
A great mistake made. So hasty.
Maybe driving you crazy?

I cheered for the cheerful.
Wept with the wailing.
And when it came to the people who wronged me,
All I wanted to do was pray for them when they were failing.
I showed mercy, whereas others perhaps would take
revenge.
I know to you it seems odd,
But no one has a better answer than GOD.

"A house divided will fall..."

- Anonymous

ILLUSIONS

Fire and ash. The two worlds that clash.
An even trade for what's worth saving,
Treasures from trash,
Better to have. Some kings are just.
Others are mad. Hours differ as life fulfills Change.
More of the same.

Interchangeable blood but different names.
Battles fought in an unfair world
As we play the ugly game.
Whose blood? Whose love?
Excuses for weakness?

Future falls in pursuits to win,
An itch for Odin's eye just to peek at the pieces.

Fellowships and alliances rise anew,
But never genuine in Lou.
Their spirit is indecent,
Wolves in sheep's clothing, the portrayal of a giver.
But underneath, they are leeches.

A number one contender for a pretender,
Just sticking around,
Smiles are frowns,
Unsettled strife, bad blood so old,
It appears brown.
War brews slowly as battle comes down.
When the clash is spent, no one's left to pick up the pieces
off the ground.

"Your journey is your journey, and don't compare it to someone else's."

— Phylicia Rashad

ANTHEM

Don't peg anybody.
Don't beg anybody.

Work if you must.
Keep your standards high.

Waste no time having seggs with anybody.
Don't be so quick to open your legs for nobody.

Listen!

Ask, and you shall receive.
Manifest while you cleave to the deeds.

Faith without works?
That's as cold and dead as corpses.

Look in the mirror,
For where the source is.

Pure and white as porcelain.

Your life choices matter as much, As your organs.

Stay on the course, sis.
It's so natural.

Don't force it.
Face it.
Don't fake it.

There's no shame in this part of the journey.
Because before you make it,
Life seems to be a never-ending fall.

Weigh around your ankles, from an anchor,
Pulling you down to the bikini bottom like plankton.

It might torture ya, but all it takes is you finding
Out what the formula is.

No matter the height you reach or who think you may know,
Always have goals.

It took me 27 years to understand
Why Janet Jackson took control.

I mean, ain't no way I'm from earth. Maybe I'm from Mars.
Even when I cried over my wounds,
I paid homage to my scars.

Good or bad,
I've gotta be one of the best children GOD ever had.
What did Michael Jackson say?

I'm Bad.

Beautiful like my mother.
Mean like my dad.

All in all, your worst is your best,
Nevertheless, remember, it's just a test.

Don't ever be afraid of a fall.
Because one thing about GOD,
He qualifies the call.

"...And I have the highest confidence ever, and I walk in the room with my head held high; regardless of if a MF likes me or not, find yourself miss..."

— Tommie Lee

MY WORLD TO ME

Why must we shun those sent to teach us?
How dangerous?
We're living in quite an era. The
World praises PickMeisha,
But demonizes Shera.
Why don't y'all hear us?
Truth is...
If you're a hater,
You're either jealous or you fear us.
Don't forget the salt with every grain.
Everything isn't for everyone,
But before I promote low self-esteem,
And raising a grown guy, I'll put your crown
On your head, I'd rather you be the prize.
Winning in a world that's already sinning.
Loving instead of hating.
Cheering and being genuine,
I'm telling you to be proud of the skin you're in.
Being taken care of through Christ is only right.
Who's perfect?
What is perfection?
The way of life is correction,
It brings me joy to see progression.
In the mornings, pray up.
Wash that face up.
Put on that makeup, because you're wonderful.

I'm proud of who I am; I just want you to be the same.
Because there's no owing when you are the trophy.
I didn't choose a confident life, the confident
Life chose me.

The apple of GODS eye.
I know because HE TOLD ME.
Royal priesthood, girl, you better know you fly.
Every mirror you see should tell you why.
Each place you walk,
Hovering over you is the sky.
It doesn't serve you to serve those who don't deserve you.
Why would you hurt yourself?
Slap yourself and go get some virtue.
If it isn't right, why would I defend it?
You have no business being with someone who has you in a
clinic.
Oh no, not the royalty, I know you are.
I'll light the way all day and night for you.
Lay to rest that trifling version of you.
Change your presentation,
Change your circle,
Change your conversation,
Next thing you know, God has blessed you,
And changed your whole situation.
Quick to hear, so shut up and listen,
Words are powerful,
Speaking wisely, only bringing life into fruition.
Be royalty.
Live royally.
Look royal.
Anointing is rare,
Get up off your bed of affliction,
Don't be scared.
Respect you so you may be the best you.
My world is my world. I'm the boss.
It's our responsibility to share all that we're taught.
I won't be responsible for misleading the lost.

PART 2

Courage: strength in the face of pain or grief.

"Courage is resistance to fear, mastery of fear, not absence of fear."

— Mark Twain

MENTAL HEALTH MANTRA: REPEAT DAILY

Dear GOD, Thank you!
For every day that you give, I know how special I am.
I matter to you.
I matter to me, and every life you will touch through me.
All my days are a love letter from you.
No matter what I may go through in life, your grace is sufficient.
I'm brilliant.
I understand that negative people are just unhappy individuals who often project their insecurities and fears onto others, and all I can do is pray for them. Releasing them.
I can't hold what I can't control.
I don't just survive, I thrive.
I release confusion.
I release doubt.
Change starts with me.
I'm capable of succeeding.
I will honor myself at every level.
I forgive myself for my shortcomings.
Small win or big; a win is a win.
I will give myself grace, Space.
I deserve peace.

Identity: the fact of being who or what a person or thing is.

STORY

Tell your story.
Stories can make you laugh or cry.
But tell me your story.
I'll tell you why.
On this earth, a being is inevitable,
But nonetheless, you are incredible.
Life has meaning beyond us,
Though and so, all those moments,
It takes to grow; it takes to know.
Shoot for the stars, reach your peak,
Go through seasons as reels,
Unfold your testimony.
Unleash.
Tell your story.
Stories can heal.
Mornings are as dew and honey as nature.
Sweet, calm, and quiet are the breezes' language,
as a wind through the birds as it takes her.
Oh, how kind of you to tell your story.
There's so much medicine in what is real.
So much strength comes from within,
Pouring out into others; something they needed to feel.
Tell me your story!
It's who you are, for all, there is purpose.
Like the sun, moon, or stars.

"...1 of 1..."

— The One

NOTE TO SELF

One of one, a diamond.
A LEO first light.
Girl, your future is so bright.
Rising from dirt,
and molding from pressure,
This effort is forever an endeavor.

Not a trick. Oh no, a treat.
For your crown is heavy,
Yet others desire your seat.

A jewel of land.
A pearl in a clam.
Persevere?
I am.

Joy instead of voids.
Life is meant to be enjoyed.
Never waste time being annoyed.

Protect your beautiful energy.
Multiply all your gifts.
You are the shit.
The Queen Bee,
27 in 26'.
You're more than legit.

You deserve an Oscar
How you prosper.

SO, Pick up your head,
Get ahead, you are brilliant.
Many pretend not to see you,
But I admire your resilience.

"I didn't come this far to come this far and not be happy."

— Anonymous

TAKE THE LEAD

What will your future cost you?
Time?
Pleasures?
Recreation?
Temporary discomfort?

Then you should also ask yourself,
How bad do you want it?

The answer is yes.
Dying out to yourself is a part of the process.
I don't think we talk enough about
What does the next level mean?

Another level means another person
It will require you to be.
What used to work won't work anymore.
It takes something else.
It's like a caterpillar becoming a butterfly,
It must spend time inside the cocoon to evolve.
Separating itself from what it would normally love.

I often hear the term "generational curse breaker". And it's quite poetic. Setting yourself apart lays a solid foundation for the future. I chose this moment to cater to the necessary conversation in life, because as much As I love dropping gems, I also believe in balance, and you should understand its importance, allowing things to digest, or better yet, manifest.

Our stories are more than a tale, but a responsibility. Big or small. Tap into who you really are. Let not who you are go to waste. You never know when you'll be someone's blessings (Or your own).

So, what say you?
Will you answer the call of GOD on your life?
Will thou be made whole?
Will time pass you as you slumber comfortably in your bed of affliction?
Will you wait when you should walk?

Each day, write a journal. Speak beautifully, calmly, and peacefully, yet affirm to yourself, speaking life. Walk in your purpose. Trust GOD.
Trust yourself. Love yourself.

JOURNAL ENTRY 1

NEW ORLEANS IN NOVEMBER:

Not even a time zone away; what a day! I'm busier than normal; my brain runs like a hamster on its wheel. With business to tend to, I managed to wake up early enough for breakfast, beignets, and a hot cup of coffee for the win. I've been thinking about my purpose lately, like a lot lately. Life has been good, great, and challenging all in one. I can perceive the future, even though tomorrow isn't promised. Optimism has me in a chokehold these days, even on the bad ones.

GOD has filled me with so much. I can feel the oil as he presses me. It runs through my spirit. As a gem, I understand, I'm hooked on Jesus's hem. I couldn't let him go if I wanted to, and with Christmas coming up, I can't think of anything other than being grateful. I mean, I am a beautiful black young woman who'd normally have a lengthy list of gift requests, but I'm just thankful. I appreciate everything. Both of my parents are still living, my grandmothers (who are the foundations of families are still going strong, and love me; my significant other loves me as well, as he shows me (that's important).

Most people miss GOD, looking at what they think is missing, while the gift of a lifetime might be right in their grasp as they're about to fumble it. Furthermore, as one might believe something is missing, it really a lot of times is themselves being impatient. GOD math may look like no to you. But is GOD saying no or not yet? Does GOD think you're ready for that? Is that for you? I learned a long time ago, never place GOD in a box, he'll move whoever he needs to out of the way to give you yours. What's for you is for you, and not a soul living can take it when GOD says so.

Anyway, things are looking up. I think I'm in the mood for a couple of slices of forbidden pizza and a night's rest.

I am the voice.

I made the choice.

– Sincerely, C. J. Henry

"...Love takes courage, even when it's for yourself..."

- Anonymous

"It's about going where you are appreciated in every way. I don't care where it is.

- Shera

"My black is beautiful, and to every other color, the feeling is mutual; every color is beautiful."
- C. J. Henry

Colorism: prejudice or discrimination against individuals with a dark skin tone, typically among people of the same ethnic or racial group.

LOVELY COLORS

The world can be cruel.
The one we live in.
It seems ironic that the most insecure
People will convince you not to love your skin.
I'm a proud black woman, GOD painted
Me, the pigment of his choice,
I've experienced my own people
Trying to silence my voice.
My best friend spoke behind me,
Saying I was too dark to walk in my shoes,
I cut negativity loose swiftly,
She went to look for me, but I left no clues.
Respond to negative actions with absence.
You don't have to be a lawyer to practice.
Teach people how to treat you, don't be a fool.
I'd rather be the villain in someone's story,
Then allow you to perceive, I'm naïve.
The skin I'm in, Oh, I know it's beautiful,
Because of my confidence?
What would you be trying to remove it for?
Misery loves competition.
However, I'm sorry to disappoint you, I'm on a mission.
So, no. I won't be attending.
A child's game of who can be more offensive.
It's beneath me.
Playing into those games would cheat me.
If I can't lift you up and you me,
Honestly, you won't even see me.
You must find someone else to lie to.
When some individuals see how great you are,
They just don't want you to know the truth.

An ugly gesture of not wanting you to see your power,
But I have no interest in anything other than God's business
We're in the last hour!
Skin?
Love what you're in.

CREATING A POSITIVE ENVIRONMENT:

1. **Understanding** – True love is about self; taking the first step is all about knowing who you are. Taking control of your world.

2. **Choose You** - The best decision I ever made was being okay with myself, enjoying my own company. I was okay with staying to myself, being out of the way, focusing on self-improvement, all while establishing a relationship with GOD because I knew only GOD could complete me. I wanted to be kept. I needed to be covered.

3. **Letting Go** – Any person, place, or thing that doesn't serve you doesn't deserve you. Learn to leave people where they are. No human being will ever have power over the next unless they hand it over. Negative thoughts or trauma must be released, and therapy is beneficial if you are willing to do the work.

4. **Changes** – Be more circumspect of what you consume. That means anything not headed in the direction GOD is bringing you. Watching negative TV shows or movies that cater to open wounds or an unfavorable persona? Change it. Listening to music catering to negative things you're trying to change about yourself? Listen to something different. Nasty Negative Backbiting, friends or family members,

always messy, no motion, not focused or tapped in with who GOD called them to be? Distance yourself. GOD has told us, "Come out from among them." Consider yourself always, meaning you could think you're strong, but whether we want to believe it or not many things are extremely influential, so show love to you, protecting peace.

5. **Action** – Write the vision. Make it plain. After writing goals and speaking affirmations, get up and move into your purpose. It's that simple. Never waste GODS time!

"...This year, I and GOD will see eye to eye..."

- C. J. Henry

PART 3

"...Silence is Golden..."

- Thomas Carlyle

SILENT SOCIETY

Be your own best friend.
You're already in the wrong place,
If you must pretend.

Be cordial if you must, pay shade with dust
But 10 times out of 10,
Close people are the ones you can't trust.

Green little bird, speak just a few words,
Silence is even better,
Some folks may appear ignorant,
But they aren't forgetters.

Tell yourself kind things,
Even if you're LY-ING!
Looking a mess in the mirror?
Stare back and say, "Go get yourself together, you fine thing."

"...Speak things as though they were" ...,
Because they have yet to appear.
As long as you're consistent,
Look forward to being 10,000 times
What you are by next year.

Announce?
No. Only confirm.
Keep running your mouth and see,
Nothing but hard ways to learn.
Evil Eyes don't get invited,
So, until you have it,
Don't recite it.
Use wisdom; it's not evil to hide it,
Be a boss and move in private.
Treat right and left hands as if they were strangers.
Now, don't let that go over your head.
It's a real game-changer.
Visions that come from GOD,
Aren't always for others around you.

Underestimate a familiar face,
They might confound you.
Open your eyes.
Pay attention to who is around you.
A reaction has power,
Even to down you.

JOURNAL ENTRY 2

SOMETIME IN JANUARY:

Each day as the sun's warmth grazes my brown skin, I feel grateful. It's so ironic, you know, the sun is shining on a star. Me. The only difference between Ikaris (who flew too close to the sun) and me is that I understand my role in humanity. I have no desire to be GOD; my desires internally are to be blessed by him. Protected. My journey with him is and has been transformative yet enlightening.

My problem is, I agree with Daenerys Targaryen. Tell me. What's the difference between her decision and GOD's? He'll destroy the world to create it again. The bible says only a remnant will be saved. The rest? Destroyed. Furthermore, I am in no way, shape, or form comparing GOD to a Targaryen; I am simply saying the concepts are similar. Our creator hates sin. Though he loves us, our sins anger him. Sin separates us from him. Nevertheless, we are just human beings, and in that way, we should be comfortable. Content. GOD's responsibility is much too hard and difficult for us anyway; beyond us even.

Circumstances show me repeatedly that I'm here for a reason. Looking back at all my challenges, as I continue to overcome, I appreciate each day GOD took to make me, break me, and build me all over again better. Greater. I treasure my scars. I wear them as jewels; on my head will always be a crown, and underneath my head, which GOD filled with tools.

I am the voice of the lost.

I am the voice of the silenced.

I am the voice of the lowly.

I am the voice.

Sincerely,

C. J. Henry

"It's not on you, it's in you, and what's in you they can't take away."

- Lauren London

JUST THOUGHTS

What happened to kindness?
Things are constantly changing.
Too many are killing,
Lord, why are they so willing?
Like really!
How chilling!
Some smiles are frowns at someone successful.
Friends becoming villains,
More voids that need filling.
Oh, how I miss the times of old.
Where women were not so bold.
Remember when children did what they were told.
Men were Men!
Head of houses, providing for their children and spouses.
Fathers were founded, rooted, and grounded,
Oh, how sweet the timing, truly astounding.
I cast no stone. I destroy no home.
Our focus should always be on ourselves.
Kings and queens to sit on their throne!
My words are life, yet the carnal folks might still gender strife.
But to hold my tongue in a time like this?
Just wouldn't be right.
I mean, really, it's trifling.
For yourself, your future, you should be fighting.
Rolling is a word, but so is time.
Utilize every moment, Analyze all components,
Cease each opportunity,
Use time wisely and continue to move quietly.
That way, when time flies, it won't pass you by.
You won't waste life working, being overworked
And underpaid, that should be a crime.

Hold on a second, let's back track quickly.
Remember when I asked, "Where's the kindness?"
Mind you, watch who you are kind to.
This world isn't fair.
Smart? Cold? Calculated?
Yea. That should be you.
A real winner controls their inner.
Get ahead so you never have to worry about bread.
So, keep these words in your head.
Never finish last because it is always up for grabs.
Manifestation, don't ever be patient.
It shall come. To have is inevitable.
Finally achieving goals feels incredible.
Show gratitude for your journey.
Love yourself every step of the way.
Have no regrets.
Always do what is best.
Ask GOD to preserve you, and you will see him have his way!

Ambition: A strong desire and determination to achieve success.

INTENTION

Scared, tired, alone.
Sweat, blood, and tears shed heavily.
Down 9. Up 10.
Hold your head up ahead.
Moving forward is certain.
The future deserves your best version.
The night sky has fallen as worlds are colliding.
Stars burst ablaze, fires of confusion and shame.
Past, present, and future show up in the flames.

Visions become truth,
As you follow through.

The energy is gloomy light.
Jade like.
Energy exchange, some to destroy,
Others to change.
Dreams? Visions?
Something tells me it is more
complicated than that.
Or maybe it's so simple,
All you need are the facts.

Though evermore clear,
The spirit speaks softly,
But only if you're willing to hear.

Rogue: denoting a person or thing that behaves in an aberrant or unpredictable way, typically with damaging or dangerous effects.

TO BE CONTINUED............

(Part 2 Coming Soon)

ABOUT THE AUTHOR

C.J. Henry is a phenomenal woman who, despite humble beginnings, never allowed her circumstances to limit her success. Thriving in her own right, she now uses her voice and poetic talent to heal, encourage, and empower others. And above all, she wholeheartedly and unapologetically shares her stories with the world.